Stock Market Build Your Basics

Analysis and Investment

Argha Ray

Copyright ©2020 Argha Ray

All rights reserved.

ISBN: 9798672624716

For You.........

Contents-

Acknowledgments

Chapter	Title	Page No.
1	Savings vs. Investments	1
2	History	7
3	Important Terms	15
4	Fundamental Analysis	25
5	Income Statement	35
6	Balance Sheet	43
7	Cash Flow Statement	51
8	Interpreting Charts	57
9	Patterns and Trends	65
10	Case Studies	93
11	Buffett's Rules	115
12	Important Notes	123
13	Mutual Funds	127
14	Scams	137
	Extras	
E1	Bonds	155
E2	Terminology	157
E3	IPO Analysis	159

Acknowledgements

Any accomplishment requires the effort of many people and this work is not different. I thank my parents whose patience and support was instrumental in accomplishing this task.

To all the individuals I have had the opportunity to lead, be led by, or watch their leadership from afar, I want to say thank you for being the inspiration and foundation for this book.

Chapter 1: Savings vs. Investments

Have you ever wondered how those insurance companies, mutual funds and other such schemes are able to give you higher returns than your bank's savings account returns?

In India, return on savings account is around 3%-4%. While average returns on FDs ranges between-

- 4% -7% for normal citizens
- 4%-8% for senior citizens

But in case of life insurance policies, mutual funds etc, they give much more than that. How is that possible? We know banks give loans to people, and share a percentage of the profit with their customers, which we get as interest on our savings. But, what about those insurance companies? Do they give loans too?

Suppose they operate like banks, they make profits through giving loans and share the profit with its customers. Note one point, they give much higher returns as compared to banks. In order to do so, they **must charge much higher interest on loans**. Then only they can afford to share such huge portion of their profits.

Now think yourself as a young entrepreneur, who needs money for a new startup. You need to get a loan for, let's say, $1,000,000. Now you have two options –

- Get the loan from a bank, or
- Get the loan from an insurance company.

Which one are you going to choose? Remember, as discussed earlier, we have assumed that insurance companies works like banks and discussed it charges much higher interest on loans. So, keeping those points in mind, definitely you are going to go for the bank, as the interest rate is much lower for the same amount of money. Even any person, who needs a loan, will go for the bank.

So, naturally, insurance companies will have no one to give loans, as a result of which, they will go bankrupt. But you see they are still active. How is that possible? Are they involved in some sort of scam? What are their sources of income then? Giving loan is definitely not an option for them. Then?

Well the answer is **STOCK MARKET**. Instead of giving loans, they invest their customers' fund in stock market. Again, note one point here, if you do a bit of research on your own, in India, banks usually charges an interest rate of around 10% on loans, then only they are able to give you a return of 3% to 4% on your savings. Similarly, insurance companies, mutual funds agencies which give a return higher as compared to banks, must be earning much more than that the amount of return they are offering, isn't it? Let's say, an insurance company gives you a return of say 9%. So, that company must be getting much higher return than that 9% from stock market, say 15%. Yes! 15%! From stock market! Much higher than your savings account return (around 3% only).

The picture is getting clear now. We get much higher return from stock market as compared to savings and fixed deposits. But, what if we directly invest in the stock market instead of any agencies? If we do so, instead of 9%, we can get a return of 15% annually! That is 12% more than that of savings account returns!

This is the reason why do we need to invest in the stock market. Now the question is, if we know that stock market gives such high returns, then why do most of the people put their money in savings account? The reason is Risk. Stock market is risky. Unlike banks, which give you an assured return, stock market doesn't give you any assurance. The interest rate in stock market varies due to various factors. The market may even crash giving you no return at all. We humans always try to avoid risks. That is why most people out there avoid investing directly or indirectly in the stock market.

Now, the question is, "Do we really need to invest in the stock market? It seems too risky!" Well, let me tell you something. Well yes, stock market is risky, I agree. But it is risky for those only who try to invest in the market without any knowledge about the market. Before we invest, we need to study and analyze the market thoroughly, select the right company for investment and other crucial factors. Analyzing the market before investing reduces the risk, even to zero. So I always encourage my readers to first learn about the market, learn how it works, how to analyze, how to select the right company in the market for investment, etc. Don't just put all your money in the market blindly.

So, now you need to learn about stock market analysis and investment. Don't worry, that's what this book is all about. There are numerous concepts involved in stock market. If you try to learn all of those, then you are always appreciated. But for us, beginners, we don't necessarily need to learn about each and everything to make a successful investment in the stock market. So we focus only on those topics which are essential for investment and analysis. This will give you more than enough knowledge for a successful investment and also save your time.

Before you proceed further, first try to understand how to read this book-

1. Once you start reading, finish the book, no matter how many days it takes.

2. Never skip any chapter.
3. After finishing every chapter you should do some more research about the topic on your own. This will keep you focused.
4. Try to understand every topic, every line, and every word very carefully and think practically. This is not a philosophical article with deep meanings, but a guide for more practical approach.
5. Once you finish this book, don't just stop, take action, otherwise there's no point of wasting your time on learning something.
6. Last rule; follow all the above mentioned rules strictly.

Chapter 2: History

"If you don't find a way to make money while you sleep, you will work until you die."

~Warren Buffett

Before we start, I would like to mention two names. First, Warren Buffett. We all have heard about this man. He is one of the richest men on Earth, chairman and CEO of Berkshire Hathaway. He is known for his brilliant skills regarding stock market. He has made most of his fortune using it. Just go and read about him. We have another person who is known as Indian Warren Buffett. His name is Rakesh Jhunjhunwala, an Indian billionaire. He has also made most of his fortune through stock market. So what is it that makes stock market so appealing? What is it that makes it so profitable?

First let's understand what stock market is and how it started. Back in 1600s, the Dutch East Indian Company used hundreds of ships to trade gold, spices, porcelain and silk. But the operations were not cheap. It required huge investments which the company couldn't afford. So they came up with a brilliant business strategy. The Company turned to private individuals or investors. The Company asked them for capital in exchange of shares of total profit. More an individual invests in the Company more the shares of profit he gets. Soon the Company started selling their shares to rich investors worldwide. In this way, the Company was able to continue their trade and also have their shares of profits. This is how the concept stock market came into existence. Although modern stock exchanges are more complex in nature, but they are all based on this base only,

Let's try to understand with an example-

- A new automobile company 'ABC' came into the market. It plans to manufacture sporty cars with engines producing huge powers. But in order to manufacture new

models they need to setup an entirely new production line which needs huge investments. So for this operation the company starts selling its shares to individual investors.
- Initially price of each share was set to Rs 100.
- Investors who saw potential in the company started buying company's shares.
- Initially when demand for shares was less, share prices were also cheap.
- Let there be a young investor Alex, who bought 100 shares for a total of Rs 10,000.
- As more and more investors started placing their orders, share prices increased. After 5 years price of each share increased to Rs 5000.
- After that, due to new emission rules, demand for electric cars increased and demand for sporty powerful cars decreased.
- Due to this, ABC was in trouble. Their sales started reducing. Thus, their share prices also started to fall.
- To avoid loss, share holders started selling their shares at Rs 5000, which was market

price of each share at that time. This gave them a profit of (Rs 5000 – Rs 100) = Rs 4900 for each share.
- Alex too sold his shares. This gave him a total profit of (100 X Rs 4900) = Rs 4,90,000.

So this is how stock market works. Alex got a profit of Rs 4,90,000 doing absolutely nothing. Thus, we can say that it is a form of passive income. But there are also some risks which are involved. Suppose the company failed in its initial days. They couldn't give you the profit that you had expected. Their share prices started falling immediately after you bought them. In that case, you get nothing but a huge amount of loss. So you need to analyze the company very well before investing in it. Don't worry, we will also discuss on how to analyze a company. Also keep in mind that it takes considerably more time to get a good amount of profit. You can also earn small amount of profits every day where you buy and sell the stocks on the same day, which is known as **intraday trade**.

Now the question is **how to buy a stock?** Stocks of different companies are traded at stock exchanges. In India, we have two major stock exchanges-

(i)   National Stock Exchange (NSE)
(ii)   Bombay Stock Exchange (BSE)

Just like to buy a new car you need to visit a dealer, similarly to buy stocks you need a broker. These are organizations that trade stocks for you in return of some brokerage. They are the certified agents of stock exchanges. In India there are several brokers, some of them even charges 0% of brokerage.

In earlier days, you could trade only through offline methods, but nowadays online modes made it much easier and faster. Earlier it took almost a month to buy or sale shares, but now, with improvements in technology, it takes a maximum time of two days.

There are myths regarding stock market investments, like- it is pure gambling, it requires high financial knowledge, only rich people can invest and so on. See, regarding gambling, definitely we cannot predict the future. No one can say what the price of a particular share price is going to be in the next moment. But in day trading, looking at the charts and patterns, one can predict to some extent if the price is going to rise or fall. For delivery of stocks or for holding of stocks for longer period of time, by analyzing past records and current overall market scenario, one can predict if a company is going to give you sufficient profit or not. Thus, it is not gambling, but if you try to invest blindly without any knowledge, without completing the book, surely it will be.

Regarding the myth- "only rich people can invest", it is completely a myth! If you do a bit of research on your own, you can see that share price of some companies are around Rs 100 only!! Anyone can afford that price.

Regarding financial knowledge, yes a bit of knowledge is required, but not like as if you need a graduation degree on finance. No matter if you are pursuing engineering, medical, arts, commerce or any other stream, anyone can learn about stock market investing, and with this book you can learn quite easily.

Alright then, dear reader, I guess you have now understood why stock market investing is better than just saving. Now it is time to proceed towards more practical knowledge.

Stock Market: Build Your Basics

Chapter 3: Important Terms

There are some terms which you will come across a lot of times while dealing with the stock market. If you start without having any sort of idea about them, you are most likely to leave the market early, lose your confidence, and might lose a great opportunity for making a good investment. So first let us understand some of those terms-

1. **Promoters-** people who had started the company.
2. **Face value-** initial value of a share. This is the price of each share when the company was established or listed itself for the first time in any stock exchange. If you remember the example of ABC Company in the previous chapter, its face value was Rs 100.
3. **Market Capital-** it is the total value of the company, or total number of shares times price of each share.
4. **Dividend-** this is the amount of money that the company gives to its share holders in

return to their investments. We will discuss more about it later.
5. **Long Term Capital Gain (L.T.C.G.)** - this is the profit that a share holder makes after selling his shares which he had kept in holding for at least 1 year.
6. **Stock Split-** when the company increases its total number of shares and decreases the share price in the same proportion.
7. **Bonus-** sometimes companies give free shares or bonus shares for free to its share holders. Similar to stock split, when bonus shares are given share price also falls in the same proportion, but face value remains unchanged. Bonus is given in a ratio like 1:1, 1:2, 2:3 etc. Suppose a company gives bonus in the ratio 2:5 which means that share holders will get 2 free shares for every 5 shares holding. For example if I have 15 shares then I will get 6 extra or bonus shares for free.
8. **IPO-** Initial Public Offering is the process of offering shares of a private company to the public in a new stock issuance. In simple words, when a private company gets listed

on the stock exchange, then the initial price of shares offered to individual investors is known as IPO. Note that a company can have only one IPO in its entire lifetime. In case of an IPO, investors cannot buy any random amount of shares; instead shares are issued in lots.

9. **FPO-** Follow-on Public Offering is the process of issuing shares to investors by a company which is already listed on the stock exchange. It is the issuance of additional shares made by a company after an IPO. Note that a company can issue more than one FPOs in its lifetime.

10. **P/E Ratio-** Price to earnings ratio is the ratio of company's share price to the company's earnings per share. It is generally used to determine whether the shares are overvalued or undervalued. If the ratio is too high, it is over price, if too low, it is undervalued.

11. **Top Line-** annual turnover or sales of the company.

12. **Bottom line** is the profit that company makes after tax.

13. **NPA-** Non Performing Assets. Sometimes, companies or individuals who had taken loans from banks go bankrupt and fail to repay the loan. In such cases those banks face huge losses and that loan adds up to their NPA. Higher the percentage of NPA, higher is the amount of loss for the bank. Thus banks always try to keep their NPA% as low as possible.
14. **Bullish-** when the share prices are rising.
15. **Bearish-** when the share prices are falling down.

Three terms- 'dividend', 'L.T.C.G.' and 'stock split' need more discussion as they are often very confusing to beginners.

Dividend-

- Dividend, as discussed earlier, is the money that a company gives to its share holders.
- Dividends are not compulsory for the companies. It is up to them whether they want to give you dividends or not.

Companies like Google, Apple etc. don't give dividends.

- It is a form of income for you. But it is **tax free up to a limit**. Try to find the current limit.
- Later on when you will start analyzing any company, if you see the company's dividend record, you may come across phrases like- '750%', '200%' etc. These percentages are put on face value.
- Suppose a company's face value is Rs 10. The market price is Rs 600. It decides to give 250% dividend to its share holders. That means it is giving Rs 25 only (250% of face value) for each share holding.

L.T.C.G.-

- It is the profit that a share holder makes after selling his shares which he has been holding for at least one year.
- It is tax free up to a certain limit.
- Remember, the share holder must hold his shares for at least one year; otherwise the profit will not be tax free.

- This is one of the reasons why long term investments are more beneficial over short term investments.

Stock Split-

- This is the situation when a company increases its total number of shares and brings down the price of each share.
- This is done to make the shares more affordable to people.
- Let us understand with the help of an example- our company, ABC, its market value is Rs 5000. Alex is holding 100 shares. So in short, the total value of Alex's shares is Rs 5,00,000. Now the ABC declares a stock split. It doubles its total number of shares and reduces the price of each share by half i.e. after stock split the market value of each stock becomes Rs 2500. Since its number of shares is doubled, thus Alex is now holding (2X100) 200 shares. Each share price is Rs 2500. So the total value of Alex's

shares is (200XRs 2500) Rs5,00,000. So the net worth remains constant.

Another small concept which you should understand is the difference between the terms 'ABC Pvt. Ltd.' and 'ABC Ltd.'

Let us again consider our company ABC.

- When it is **'ABC Pvt. Ltd.'**, it is a private company.
- It is not listed on any stock exchange.
- Only its **promoters** can invest in it i.e. buy or sell its share.
- When it is **'ABC Ltd.'**, it is a public company.
- It is now listed on stock exchanges.
- Anyone can now invest in the company.
- This is done when more funding is required for the company.

Short Selling

The basic trading strategy or principle is to first buy shares at a lower price and then sell them at a higher price to get the profit. But alternatively, one can first sell stocks at a higher rate (even when the trader has no shares at all) and then buy them back when the price falls. It sounds confusing, so let us understand by an example-

- Suppose you enter the market for intraday trading. Initially you have no shares at all. Suppose you are planning to look for trading with shares of 'ABC' company.
- When you try to analyse the chart, you find that the share price is going to fall. You cannot place a buy order at that time because that will lead to pure loss. So you put a sell order first. Let's say you place a sell order for 5 shares with current share price of Rs 150 each. So, the total number of shares you have now is '-5'.
- Later on when the price falls to Rs 100, you buy the shares back. So now you have (-5+5) = 0 number of shares.
- So ultimately, you buy shares at Rs 100 each, and sell them at Rs 150 each. So you get a profit of 5X(150-100)= Rs 250. This is the concept of short selling.
- Short selling is not allowed in some countries. Although Indian Government

allows it only in intraday trading case and not for delivery.
- Short selling is considered to be more risky than normal trading.

These are some basic terms which one should know before entering the market. There are many other terms which are more advanced, like 'stop loss', 'resistance', 'support' etc. which you will get to know once you enter the market.

In the next chapter we are going to discuss about methods of analyzing a company before investing. But before, revise the terms and concepts discussed once again.

Chapter 4: Fundamental Analysis

Before we make any investment in stock market, we must first select the company/ companies whose stocks we are going to buy. For that we need to develop some basic skills for analyzing stocks and figure out whether they are going to give you high returns or not. Remember, when you buy a share of any company you are actually buying a part of company's ownership an. So if the profit is in negative i.e. if the company faces a loss you are going to face that loss. Therefore it is highly recommended to analyze carefully and figure out whether the company is performing well or not.

There are some important rules which you should keep in mind before getting started with stock market-

1. Don't enter the stock market blindly.
2. As suggested by Warren Buffett, invest only in those stocks which you understand.

3. Don't put all your money at once.
4. Start with that much amount of money which you can afford to lose.
5. Go for long term investments. They give higher returns with minimum risk. Short term investments are very risky.

These rules are meant for beginners. Once you become an expert you can you can start making new strategies of your own, but make sure that you never lose money.

To begin analysis, visit your broker and get access to a company's annual report. These data are available online. I would recommend **Money Control.** This website is free and you don't need to even register in the website for any action.

Visit- "**www.moneycontrol.com**" and look for **Corp Action**" and "**Financials**" tabs. Under these sections you will get the technical data required. Two forms of data available there- **Standalone** and **Consolidated.** Now the question is, which form of data do we actually need? To answer this question, let us understand what exactly standalone and consolidated data mean.

Standalone- when several companies operate under one single parent company, in such cases those individual companies are called subsidiary companies of the parent company. Now if those subsidiary companies are listed on the stock exchange then they must be big companies and their performances directly influence the parent company's performance. In such cases analyzing only the parent company won't be very beneficial. In such cases we need to read and study the **standalone** data of those subsidiary companies. For example, HDFC is a parent company, but it has HDFC bank, HDFC life insurance and several other companies under it which are listed on the stock exchange. Standalone data gives the data for one particular business.

Consolidated- there are several companies which operate under one parent company, but are not listed on the stock exchange although the parent company is listed. In such cases, consolidated data for the parent company is required. Consolidated data gives the overall performance data for any particular company.

There, look for the following fundamental data-

1. Top line
2. Profit
3. Bottom line
4. Share price

Year->	1	2	3	4	5
Top line					
Profit					
Bottom line					
Share price					

Top line is the annual turnover or sales of the company. **Bottom line** is the profit that company makes after tax. After you have collected the above data, follow these steps-

1. Compare last five years annual report of the company.
2. Know about its future aspects. Read about the company's future plans and expectations.
3. Compare and understand the current market. Make sure that the company will perform well in the current market scenario.
4. Make sure that the top line is increasing.
5. Make sure that the bottom line is increasing faster than the top line. If this happens, it is a good indication that it will give you high returns.
6. If the share price suddenly falls down, check if it is due to stock split or not.
7. Check the volume of shares traded. It should be very high, which means a lot of investors are interested in this company. So the risk is less.

8. For banks, also check the NPA history. For a good banking performance NPAs must be very low.

These are some basic analysis which anyone, irrespective of his/her education level, can do. You don't need a very high finance education for this. Also, if you go through the prices of shares, you will instantly realize that they are actually very affordable. You don't need to be a very rich man before your first trade. Yes, you may say it is risky. But it is not pure gambling. Stock market is based on you understanding of market and analysis. If you can do some research and analyze well, you can predict the trend and also reduce the risk.

Many a times, after investing, share price begins to fall down. In that case the investor loses all his hope and out of regret sells his shares with huge losses. This is one the mistakes that beginners make. Remember, **history repeats itself**. If the market crashes share prices fall down, don't just give up. Remember what we said earlier? Long term investments are always profitable. If the market crashes, after some time it bounces back. There are two case studies on analysis of stocks in chapter 7, so that you can get a good idea on how it is done

Index Funds-

Sometimes, instead of buying shares of companies, investors invest in index funds. For NSE it is **Nifty50**, while for BSE, it is **Sensex**. Nifty50 consists of 50 top performing companies listed on NSE. Sensex consists of 30 top performing companies listed on BSE.

You can think of index fund as a company. It has shares for sale with a share price. Take the example of Nifty50. If you buy a share of Nifty50, your money will get distributed to all those 50 companies listed under it. Price of shares is used to understand the overall performance of the market. Similar is the case of Sensex.

Now what if some of these companies under Nifty goes bankrupt or fails? In that case, to minimize the loss, those companies are replaced by companies ranked just below these companies. Putting money in index funds actually reduces the risk. Index funds often give very high returns. For example, if we consider the case of Nifty, if you do a bit of research, on an average, it gives an annual return of around 15%, which is actually a pretty good number. There will a separate chapter with case studies on fundamental analysis of some real-time companies.

The method discussed in this chapter is for basic analysis. It gives you a basic idea about a company's performance. There are some mid cap and small cap companies that have huge potentials for growth. Investing in such companies are risky, but also the expected returns are very high. Experienced investors often invest in such companies. In order to make sure that the company will perform well, investors use **Financial Statements** to analyse the company. Analysis of financial statements is an advanced stage of fundamental analysis. In upcoming chapters we are going to discuss about the three components of financial statement, i.e. income statement, balance sheet and cash flow statement.

Chapter 5: Income Statement

Financial statements are official record of all the financial activities of a business. It is mandatory for all companies to publish their financial statements to public. There are three components of financial statements- income statement, balance sheet and cash flow statement. Let's begin with income statement.

Definition- Income statement, also known as profit and loss statement, is a document which summarizes a company's profit and expenses over a period of time (quarterly or annually). As discussed in the previous chapter, top line, profit, and bottom line are actually a part of income statement or profit and loss statement. Income statements come in two formats- **Single Step** and **Multi Step**.

Single Step Format includes-

1. Net sale (top line)
2. Materials and production
3. Marketing and administration

4. Research and development expenses (R&D)
5. Other income and expenses
6. Pretax income
7. Taxes
8. Net income (after tax or bottom line)

Note

- Gross income=
  (net sales) - (materials and production)
- Operating income=
  (gross income) - (R&D) - (marketing and administration)

Multi Step Format includes-

1. Net sales (top line)
2. Cost of sales
3. Gross income
4. Selling, general and administrative expenses (SG&A)
5. Operating Income
6. Other income and expenses
7. Pretax income

8. Taxes
9. Net income (after tax or bottom line)

- **Net sales-** the net value of a company's sales of its good s and services.
- **Cost of sales-** for a manufacturer, cost of sales are the expenses involved in manufacturing of the product including cost of raw materials, labors, machineries and other production related expenses. For service related business, cost of sales are the expenses involved in the service. For retailers, cost of sales involves the cost for purchasing of products from supplier or manufacturer.
- **Gross profit-** it is calculated by subtracting cost of sales from net sales, i.e.
  Gross profit= (net sales) - (cost of sales)
- **Selling, general and administrative expenses (SG&A)-** these are company's operational expenses, like wages of employees, rental bills, etc.

- **Operating income-** it is the company's earnings from its normal operations. It is calculated as-
  Operating income= (gross profit) - (SG&A)
  This data is very important for analysts as it excludes taxes and other non operating incomes or expenses, hence give a very clear picture of a company's overall performance.

How to use Income Statement

To read the income statement, we use the data given to calculate some financial ratios. Such ratios are used to understand the current position of the company and also compare the company with other companies. Following are most commonly used income statement ratios-

1. **Gross margin-** it is the percentage of sales revenues available for profit after the cost of sales is deducted.
   Gross margin= (gross profit)/(net sales)
2. **Profit margin-** it is the ratio of net profit after tax (or bottom line) to net sales.

Profit margin= (net profit after tax)/(net sales)

3. **Operating margin-** it is the ratio of operating income to net sales. It represents how well the company manages it returns.
   Operating margin= (operating income)/(net sales)
4. **Earnings per share (EPS)-** it is a very crucial ratio for investors and analysts. It indicates the amount of profit that the company makes per share.
   EPS= (net income)/(total number of company's shares)
5. **Price- Earnings (P/E) ratio-** another crucial ratio for stock valuation, P/E ratio determines whether the shares are overvalued or undervalued. If the ratio is too high, it is over price, if too low, it is undervalued. P/E ratio is calculated by dividing the share price by earnings per share.
   P/E= (share price)/(EPS)
6. **Times interest earned (TIE) ratio-** this ratio represents a company's ability to repay its debts. Higher the TIE ratio better is the

company. A TIE greater than 2.5 is considered an acceptable risk.

These are some ratios commonly used by investors and analysts to understand the income statement and compare companies.

NOTE

While using financial statements and its ratios to compare different companies, always compare those companies which fall under the same sector or category or industry. For example, you should compare an automobile company with another automobile company, and not IT companies.

Following is the annual income statement of Maruti Suzuki India for the financial year 2019-20. Try to calculate the ratios discussed above from the given data-

Stock Market: Build Your Basics

Statement of Profit and Loss
for the year ended March 31, 2020

(All amounts in ₹ million, unless otherwise stated)

Particulars	Notes No.	Page No.	For the Year ended 31.03.2020	For the Year ended 31.03.2019
I Revenue from operations	22	236	756,106	860,203
II Other income	23	236	34,208	25,610
III Total Income (I+II)			790,314	885,813
IV Expenses				
Cost of materials consumed	24.1	237	346,366	450,239
Purchases of stock-in-trade			187,581	143,138
Changes in inventories of finished goods, work-in-progress and stock-in-trade	24.2	237	(2,381)	2,108
Employee benefits expenses	25	237	33,839	32,549
Finance costs	26	238	1,329	758
Depreciation and amortisation expenses	27	238	35,257	30,189
Other expenses	28	238-239	118,892	123,397
Vehicles / dies for own use			(1,217)	(1,221)
Total expenses (IV)			719,666	781,157
V Profit before tax (III - IV)			70,648	104,656
VI Tax expense				
Current tax	29	239-240	13,748	29,323
Deferred tax	29	239-240	394	327
			14,142	29,650
VII Profit for the year (V - VI)			56,506	75,006
VIII Other Comprehensive Income				
A (i) Items that will not be reclassified to profit or loss				
(a) gain / (loss) of defined benefit obligation	14.4	230-231	(718)	(435)
(b) gain / (loss) on change in fair value of equity instruments	14.5	231	(3,902)	(1,745)
			(4,620)	(2,180)
A (ii) Income tax relating to items that will not be reclassified to profit or loss	29	239-240	203	149
B (i) Items that will be reclassified to profit or loss				
(a) effective portion of gain / (loss) on hedging instruments in a cash flow hedge	14.6	231	-	2
			-	2
B (ii) Income tax relating to items that will be reclassified to profit or loss	29	239-240	-	(1)
Total Other Comprehensive Income (A (i+ii)+B (i+ii))			(4,417)	(2,030)
IX Total Comprehensive Income for the year (VII + VIII)			52,089	72,976
Earnings per equity share (₹)	31	241		
Basic			187.06	248.30
Diluted			187.06	248.30

The accompanying notes are forming part of these financial statements

Chapter 6: Balance Sheet

Balance sheet is an official document which gives detailed information about a company's assets and liabilities. In short, **Assets** are those items that are owned by the company or generate income for the company, like any building, cars or machineries owned by the company. On the other hand, **Liabilities** are those items which take money out of the company, like any loan from bank or other borrowings.

In a balance sheet, total value of assets is always balanced by total value of liabilities. This is represented by the following equation-

Assets = Liabilities + Shareholder's Equity

Like we know, to raise funds, a company can use two methods. First, by taking loans from banks, bonds and other sources, this adds up to liabilities. Second, by selling its shares, this adds up to share holder's equity.

Balance sheets should be compared with those of previous periods and also with those of other businesses in the same industry.

Assets

Under the asset section, different types of assets are listed in order of their liquidity, that is, the ease with which they can be converted to cash. That means assets which can be most easily converted to cash is placed at the top, and the most difficult ones are placed at the bottom. There are two main categories of assets-

1. **Current assets-** assets that can be converted to cash within a year.
2. **Non-current assets/Long term assets-** assets that take more than one year to be converted in to cash.

Note-

Balance sheets of different companies might contain different forms of assets under current and non-current assets. So, in this chapter, we will have a discussion on general order of accounts within current and non-current assets.

Types of Current Assets-

1. **Cash and cash equivalents-** these are most liquid assets which can include hard cash as well as short term certificates of deposits.
2. **Marketable securities-** this category includes equity and debt securities for which there is a market.
3. **Accounts receivable-** sometimes, companies especially manufacturers give their customers some time to pay the money. This due amount is included in this category.
4. **Inventory-** this is the total value of goods which are available for sale.
5. **Prepaid expenses-** these are expenses or the amount of money that has already been paid for such as insurance, advertisements etc. Now, as the name suggests it is an expense, then why it is included in assets? This is because these are expenses that

have not yet expired. As it expires, the asset is reduced.

Types of Non-Current Assets-

1. **Fixed assets-** these include mostly tangible items like land, machineries, buildings, cars, etc which are owned by the company.
2. **Intangible assets-** these includes assets which cannot be touched such as patents, trademarks, copyrights, internet domains, software, etc which are owned by the company.

Liabilities

Liabilities include the amount of money that the company owes to outside parties such as loans, interests to be paid on bonds, due bills to be paid to suppliers, rent, salaries, etc. Just like assets, there are two main categories of liabilities-

1. **Current liabilities-** those which are due within one year.
2. **Non-current/Long term liabilities-** liabilities which are due after one year.

Types of Current Liabilities-

1. Current portion of long term debt
2. Bank indebtedness
3. Wages
4. Customer repayments
5. Dividends to be paid and others
6. Earned and unearned premiums
7. Accounts payable

Types of Non-Current Liabilities-

1. **Long term debts-** these include interest and principle on bonds issued by the company.
2. **Pension fund-** this is the money that a company pays to its retired employees.
3. **Deferred tax-** these are the taxes that will not be paid for another year.

Share Holder's Equity

Share holder's equity is also called **net assets** as it is equal to the total assets of the company minus its liabilities. It is the money of business owners or share holders.

Note

- **Retained earnings-** these are the net earnings of a company which it reinvests in the company or give back to its shareholders in the form of dividends.
- **Treasury stocks-** these are the stocks of the company which it has repurchased, which can be sold later to raise cash.

How to use Balance Sheet

Similar to the case of income statement, to study and analyse balance sheets we use some financial ratios. Following are the most commonly used financial ratios used to study any balance sheet and compare different companies-

1. **Return on assets ratio-** this ratio gives then net return per asset value.
   Return on assets= (net pretax profit)/(total assets)
2. **Debt to equity (D/E) ratio-** this is one of the most crucial ratio in the entire analysis activity. D/E ratio tells us how well a company is financing its operations. It is calculated as-
   D/E= (total liabilities)/(shareholder's equity)
   Higher D/E ratio indicates higher risks and vice-versa.
3. **Current ratio-** this ratio is used to determine a company's ability to payback its short term obligations or short term liabilities.

These are some ratios commonly used by investors and analysts to understand the balance sheet and compare companies. Following is the balance sheet of Maruti Suzuki India for the financial year 2019-20. Try to calculate the ratios discussed above from the given data-

Stock Market: Build Your Basics

Balance Sheet
As at March 31, 2020

(All amounts in ₹ million, unless otherwise stated)

Particulars	Notes No.	Page No.	As at 31.03.2020	As at 31.03.2019
ASSETS				
Non-current assets				
Property, plant and equipment	4	221-222	147,618	149,567
Capital work-in-progress	4	221-222	13,374	16,001
Intangible assets	5	223	4,067	4,511
Right-of-use Assets	35	258-259	6,127	-
Financial assets				
Investments	6	223-226	352,488	314,695
Loans	7	226	2	2
Other financial assets	9	227	358	340
Other non-current assets	12	228	17,213	20,586
Total non-current assets			541,247	505,702
Current assets				
Inventories	10	227	32,149	33,257
Financial assets				
Investments	6	223-226	12,188	50,455
Trade receivables	8	226	21,270	23,104
Cash and bank balances	11	228	211	1,789
Loans	7	226	169	160
Other financial assets	9	227	5,075	4,964
Current tax assets (Net)	21	235	5,269	4,274
Other current assets	12	228	7,943	5,613
Total current assets			84,274	123,616
Total Assets			**625,521**	**629,318**
EQUITY AND LIABILITIES				
Equity				
Equity share capital	13	228-229	1,510	1,510
Other equity	14	229-232	482,860	459,905
Total equity			484,370	461,415
Liabilities				
Non-current liabilities				
Financial liabilities				
Lease liabilities	35	258-259	550	-
Provisions	17	233-234	516	395
Deferred tax liabilities (Net)	18	234	5,984	5,640
Other non-current liabilities	19	235	21,153	20,365
Total non-current liabilities			28,203	26,400
Current liabilities				
Financial liabilities				
Borrowings	15	232	1,063	1,406
Trade payables				
Total outstanding dues of micro and small enterprises	20	235	478	682
Total outstanding dues of creditors other than micro and small enterprises	20	235	74,463	95,648
Lease liabilities	35	258-259	94	-
Other financial liabilities	16	232	9,017	14,400
Provisions	17	233-234	6,796	6,244
Current tax liabilities (Net)	21	235	6,982	6,729
Other current liabilities	19	235	14,075	16,304
Total current liabilities			112,948	141,503
Total liabilities			**141,151**	**167,903**
Total Equity and Liabilities			**625,521**	**629,318**

The accompanying notes are forming part of these financial statements

Chapter 7: Cash Flow Statement

A cash flow statement gives us detailed information about cash and cash equivalents entering or leaving a company. Cash flow statements shows how well a company can generate cash to fund its operations, pay its debts, and overall profit.

Any cash flow statement consists of three main components-

1. Cash from operating activities
2. Cash from investing activities
3. Cash from financial activities

Cash from Operating Activities

This category includes any sources of cash related directly to the main business activities. In simple words, cash from operating activities is the cash that a company makes by its products and services. Different companies might have different sub-categories under cash from operating activities section. In general cash from operating activities includes-

1. Receipts from sales of goods and services.
2. Interest payments.
3. Income tax payments.
4. Payments made to suppliers.
5. Salary and wage payments.
6. Rent payments.
7. Other operating expenses.

Cash from Investing Activities

This includes the amount of cash a company uses for its investments. For example- buying or selling of any property like land, buildings, cars or any other assets, loans made to vendors or received from customers, etc.

Cash from Financial Activities

This category includes cash from sources like investors or banks. It also includes cash paid to shareholders as dividends, repayment of debt principles, stock repurchases etc.

NOTE

In some cases the overall cash flow might be negative. Although it generally indicates that the company is in loss, but sometimes that might not be the case. A negative cash flow can also be the result of the company's decision to expand its business at a certain point of time. This could be a good thing in the future. Investors and analysts always study and analyse previous years' cash flow statements also to get a better idea about the company's performances.

How to use Cash Flow Statements

To study a cash flow statement investors and analysts generally use three ratios-

1. **Cash flow to sales-** this ratio helps us to determine how much money a company generates for each unit of sales. It is calculated as-

Cash flow to sales= (cash from operating activities)/(net sales)

2. **Operating index-** - this ratio helps us to determine how much money a company generates for each unit of net income after tax. It is calculated as-

   Operating index= (cash from operating activities)/(net income after tax)

3. **Operating cash flow ratio-** this ratio is another important ratio which tells us whether the company is able to generate enough cash to cover its current liabilities. It is calculated as-

   Operating cash flow ratio= (cash from operating activities)/(current liabilities)

   Note that if this ratio falls below 1 then the company is not making enough cash from its core business activities, which is not a good sign.

Following is the cash flow statement of Maruti Suzuki India for the financial year 2019-20. Try to calculate the ratios discussed above from the given data-

Cash Flow Statement
for the year ended March 31, 2020

(All amounts in ₹ million, unless otherwise stated)

Particulars	Notes No.	Page No.	For the Year ended 31.03.2020	For the Year ended 31.03.2019
A Cash flow from Operating Activities:				
Profit before tax			70,648	104,656
Adjustments for:				
Depreciation and amortisation expense	27	238	35,257	30,189
Finance costs	26	238	1,329	758
Interest income	23	236	(966)	(1,237)
Dividend income	23	236	(904)	(91)
Net loss on sale / discarding of property, plant and equipment	28	238-239	424	531
Net gain on sale of investments in debt mutual funds	23	236	(1,503)	(1,601)
Fair valuation gain on investment in debt mutual funds	23	236	(29,413)	(22,681)
Liabilities no longer required written back	22	236	(37)	(53)
Unrealised foreign exchange (gain)/ loss			(766)	85
Operating Profit before Working Capital changes			74,067	110,556
Adjustments for changes in Working Capital :				
- (Increase)/decrease in other financial assets (non-current)	9	227	(18)	(16)
- (Increase)/decrease in other non-current assets	12	228	(1,549)	(4,281)
- (Increase)/decrease in inventories	10	227	1,108	(1,649)
- (Increase)/decrease in trade receivables	8	226	1,888	(8,518)
- (Increase)/decrease in loans (current)	7	226	(9)	(130)
- (Increase)/decrease in other financial assets (current)	9	227	808	(2,155)
- (Increase)/decrease in other current assets	12	228	(2,416)	7,506
- Increase/(decrease) in non-current provisions	17	233-234	121	130
- Increase/(decrease) in other non-current liabilities	19	235	788	4,512
- Increase/(decrease) in trade payables	20	235	(21,551)	(8,603)
- Increase/(decrease) in other financial liabilities (current)	16	232	(2,576)	4,501
- Increase/(decrease) in current provisions	17	233-234	(166)	209
- Increase/(decrease) in other current liabilities	19	235	(2,067)	(4,702)
Cash generated from Operating Activities			48,408	97,360
- Income taxes paid (net)			(14,357)	(31,428)
Net Cash from / (used in) Operating Activities			34,051	65,932
B Cash flow from Investing Activities:				
Payments for purchase of property, plant and equipment and capital work in progress	4	221-222	(31,936)	(47,447)
Payments for purchase of intangible assets	5	223	(2,423)	(1,254)
Proceeds from sale of property, plant and equipment	4	221-222	369	1,701
Payments for purchase of investment in Associate/JV company	6	223-226	(150)	(3)
Proceeds from sale of debt mutual funds	6	223-226	469,687	539,864
Payments for purchase of debt mutual funds	6	223-226	(442,050)	(529,572)
Interest received	23	236	960	1,237
Dividend received	23	236	904	91
Net Cash from / (used in) Investing Activities			(4,639)	(35,383)

Cash Flow Statement
for the year ended March 31, 2020

(All amounts in ₹ million, unless otherwise stated)

Particulars	Notes No.	Page No.	For the Year ended 31.03.2020	For the Year ended 31.03.2019
C Cash flow from Financing Activities:				
Movement in short term borrowings (net)	15	232	(433)	388
Principal elements of lease payments	35	258-259	(91)	-
Finance cost paid	26	238	(1,342)	(732)
Payment of dividend on equity shares	14.4	230-231	(24,166)	(24,166)
Related income tax	14.4	230-231	(4,968)	(4,968)
Net Cash from / (used in) Financing Activities			(31,000)	(29,478)
Net Increase/(Decrease) in cash & cash equivalents			(1,588)	1,071
Cash and cash equivalents at the beginning of the year			1,770	699
Cash and cash equivalents at the end of the year			182	1,770
Cash and cash equivalents comprises :				
Cash and cheques in hand	11	228	1	881
Balance with Banks	11	228	181	889
			182	1,770
Other bank balances - unclaimed dividend accounts	11	228	29	19
Cash and Bank balances	11	228	211	1,789

The accompanying notes are forming part of these financial statements

Chapter 8: Interpreting Charts

Line Chart

Stock Market: Build Your Basics

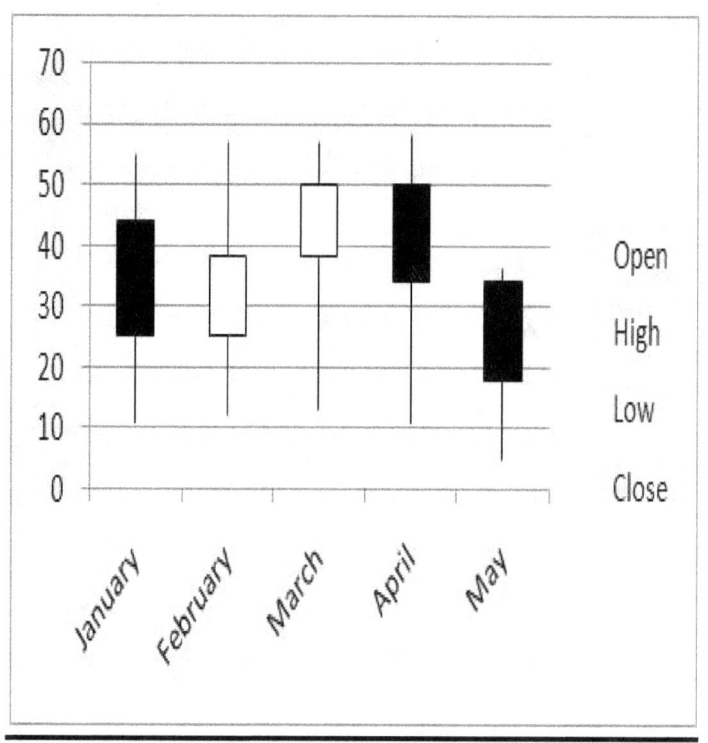

Candle Stick Chart

There are several charts which are available out there. But the most commonly used charts are- **line chart** and **candle stick chart**, which are shown in the previous page.

Now, what exactly is a chart? It is basically a graphical representation of share prices of a company. Various charts show various information but most of the time we need information like open price, close price, highest and lowest prices.

A line chart shows the closing price only but a candle stick chart shows all of the above information, so it is the most ideal chart that we can use. If you visit any broker's website, after you search for company, it will immediately show you the chart of the company. Using this chart we can decide when we need to buy the shares or sell them.

NOTE

- **Open price-** price of each share at the time of market opening,
- **Close price-** price of each share at the time of market closing.
- **High-** high or today's high is the highest price of each share on a particular day.
- **Low-** low or today's low is the lowest price of each share on a particular day.

Line Chart-

In the beginning of this chapter, we came across a typical line chart. Each point on the chart represents the closing price of stock at that moment. Since it shows only very little information, investors don't use this type of chart very often. Most investors seek the help of candle stick chart.

Candle Stick-

In candle stick chart, you may notice 'candle sticks' as shown below-

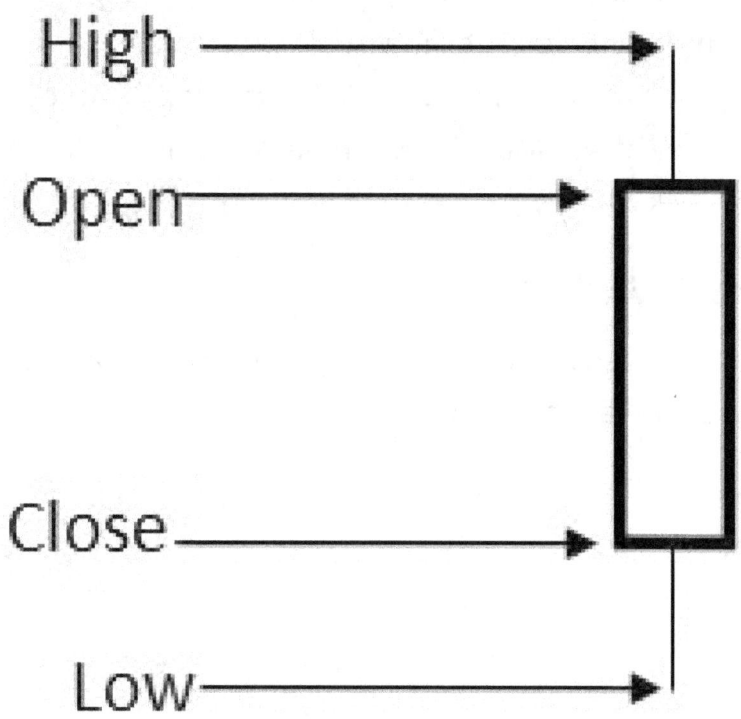

This chart is more convenient as 4 different data can be represented through this. You can notice that there are two kinds of candle sticks on a chart- red coloured and green coloured. The red coloured candle is a bearish candle which means prices are falling down. A green coloured candle is a bullish candle which means the prices are rising up.

By reading the charts we can decide when to buy or when to sell our shares. The key rule is to buy the shares at lower rates and sell them at high rates.

Importance of charts in 'Intraday Trading'

Earlier we have discussed about long term investment, its benefits, its rules etc. But stock market can also be used to make small profits within a day. This is called **intraday trading**, where you buy and sell the stocks within the same day.

If you are planning for an intraday trade you must have a very good knowledge on how to read the charts and understand its patterns and trends. This is because to earn maximum profit, you need to predict when the prices are going to be high or low. Then only you can place an order at a low price and make profit by selling your shares at a high price. This is quite difficult and risky, but if you can identify and understand the patterns you can reduce the risk. Therefore chart reading and understanding its patterns and trends are so important.

In the next chapter we are going to discuss about chart patterns and trends. But before that, please go through some charts of any company and try to understand them on your own.

Chapter 9: Patterns and Trends

We learnt how to read a chart. Now let's talk about some trends in stock market which you can observe every day.

- Stock market opens and closes at fixed times. In India, market opens at 9.15 am and closes t 3.30 pm and for five days a week (Monday – Friday).
- Trade can also be carried after the market gets closed. These are aftermarket transactions. You can trade but they are not executed until the market opens.
- All the aftermarket trades are executed once the market opens.
- When market opens, one can observe that the market is very volatile. Share prices vary very much. This is because all the aftermarket trades get executed at that time. Beginners are usually advised not to trade during this high volatility period.
- Once this high volatility period is over, the chart starts showing identifiable patterns.

These are some of the most common trends which you will come across while trading. Now let's talk about some of the patterns which our charts may show. There are three kinds of pattern which we will discuss here-

1. Triangle
2. Double tops and double bottoms
3. Rectangle

Triangle-

If you carefully observe the a chart, let's say a line chart, you may sometimes observe a the lines are forming a triangle shape, as shown below-

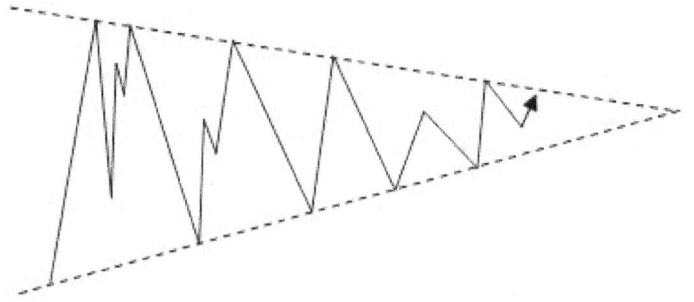

Stock Market: Build Your Basics

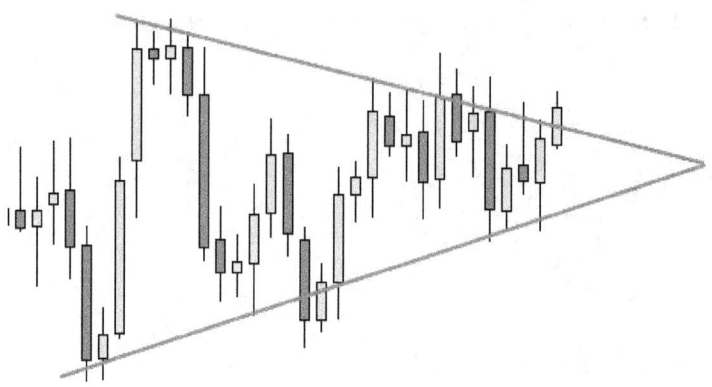

This is a typical example of triangle pattern. It represents a zone of contracting volatility and indecision wherein neither the buyer nor the seller are able to push the price in any particular direction. Three types of triangles are there-

I. Symmetrical triangle
II. Ascending triangle
III. Descending triangle

Symmetrical Triangle-

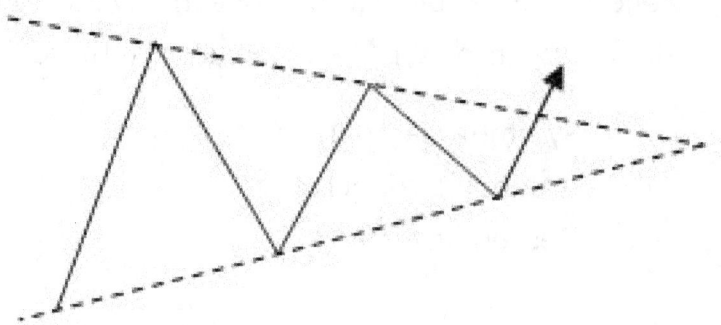

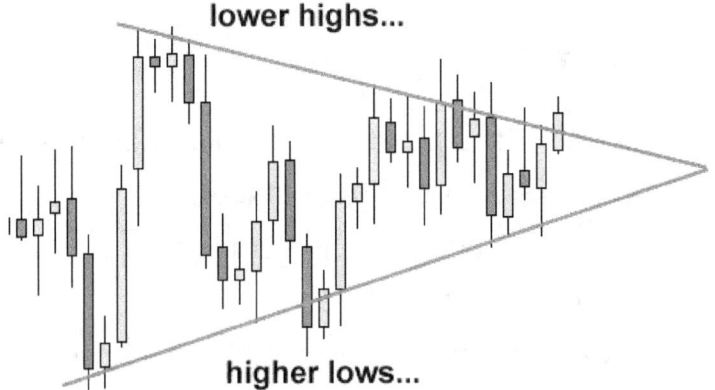

Features-

- Higher lows.
- Lower highs.

Explanation-

- Represents a period of consolidation before the price is forced to breakout.
- Breakdown from the lower trend line represents bearish trend.
- Breakout from upper trend line represents bullish trend.
- The pattern can range from a few weeks to an average of 1-3 months.

Trading-

- Entry is taken when the price breaks out.
- Price projection method is very widely used in such case.
- Take the distance between the high and the low of the symmetrical triangle, the widest point of the pattern.
- Add it to the breakout point. That is your target price.

- For example, let at the start the low be Rs 100 and move up to Rs 150. Breakout occurs at Rs 120. Then the target price is (150-100+120)= Rs 170.
- Buy at the breakout and sell at the target price.

Ascending Triangle-

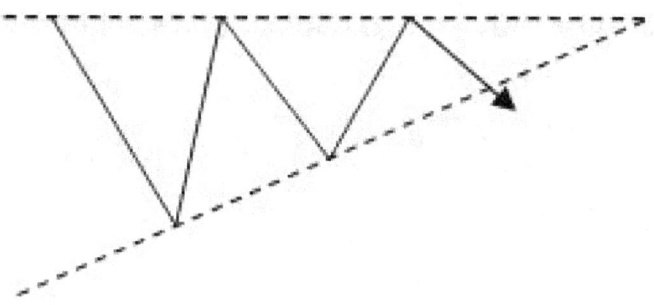

Features-

- Bullish.
- Higher lows.
- Flat highs (constant high).

Explanation-

- Two or more equal highs form a horizontal line (resistance) at the top.
- The highs need not to be exactly equal, but should be reasonably close in values.
- Also, there should be considerable amount of gap between these highs.
- Two or more rising troughs form an ascending trend line that converges with the horizontal line (resistance) as it rises.
- The pattern can range from a few weeks to an average of 1-3 months.
- The horizontal line indicates that a large sell order has been placed which is taking a lot of time to execute, which prevents the price from rising further.

Trading-

- Entry is taken when the price breaks out.

- Buy when the breakout takes place at upper side.
- Sell or short sell if breakout takes place at downside.

Descending Triangle-

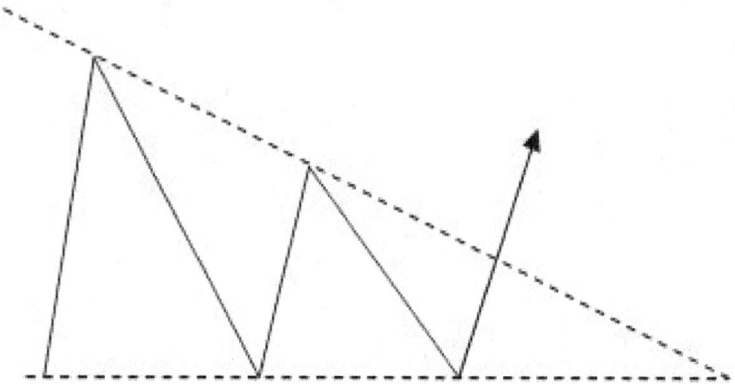

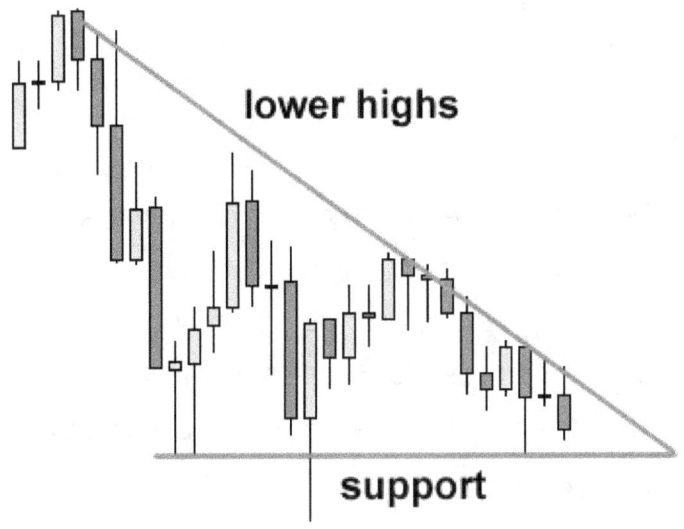

Features-

- Bearish.
- Lower highs.
- Flat lows.

Explanation-

- Two or more equal lows form a horizontal line (support) at the top.
- The lows need not to be exactly equal, but should be reasonably close in values.
- Also, there should be considerable amount of gap between these lows.
- Two or more falling troughs form an descending trend line that converges with the horizontal line (support) as it rises.
- The pattern can range from a few weeks to an average of 1-3 months.
- The horizontal line indicates that a large buy order has been placed which is taking a lot of time to execute, which prevents the price from declining further.

Trading-

- Entry is taken when the price breaks out.

- Buy when the breakout takes place at upper side.
- Sell or short sell if breakout takes place at downside.

Double Tops and Double Bottoms-

- These are reversal patterns usually acquiring over a larger time interval.
- 'M' and 'W' shapes can be observed.
- Double top should be preceded with a bullish trend, while a double bottom should be preceded with a bearish trend.

Double Top-

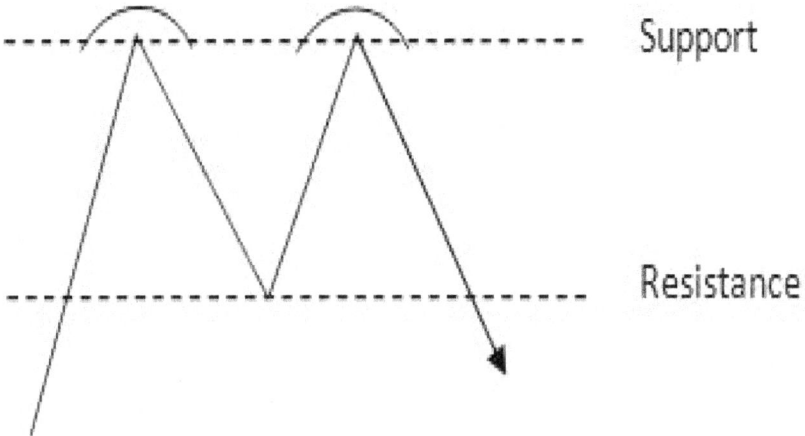

Stock Market: Build Your Basics

Features-

- Looks like the letter "M".
- Bearish reversal pattern.
- Found on line charts, bar charts and candlestick charts.

Explanation-

- Made up of two consecutive peaks which are equal or nearly equal with moderate troughs in between.
- Significant uptrend of considerable number of months should be there before.
- Peaks should be separated by considerable distance.
- The decline from peak must be a least 10%.

Trading-

- Entry is made when the trend is broken.
- This trend is highly reversible, hence place orders accordingly.
- Sell/ short sell when the trend breaks.

Double Bottom-

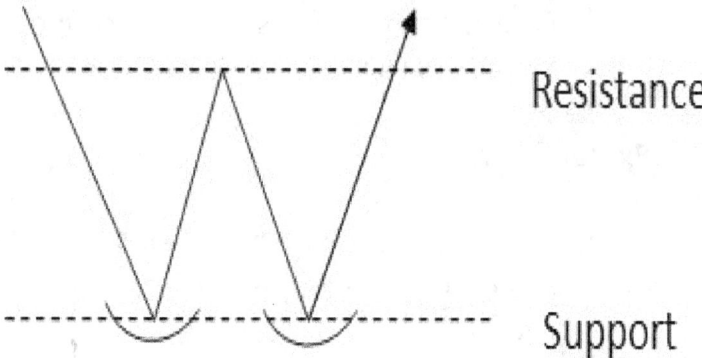

Features-

- Looks like the letter "W".
- Bullish reversal pattern.
- Found on line charts, bar charts and candlestick charts.

Explanation-

- Made up of two consecutive troughs which are equal or nearly equal with moderate troughs in between.
- Significant downtrend of considerable number of months should be there before.
- Peaks should be separated by considerable distance.
- The advance from trough must be a least 10%.

Trading-

- Entry is made when the trend is broken.
- This trend is highly reversible, hence place orders accordingly.
- Buy when the trend breaks.

Rectangle-

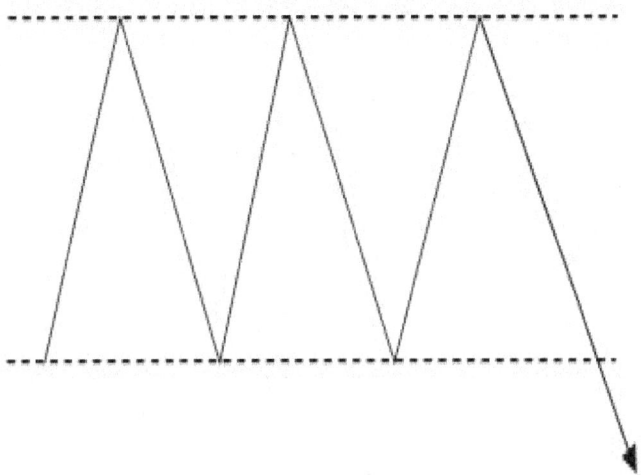

Stock Market: Build Your Basics

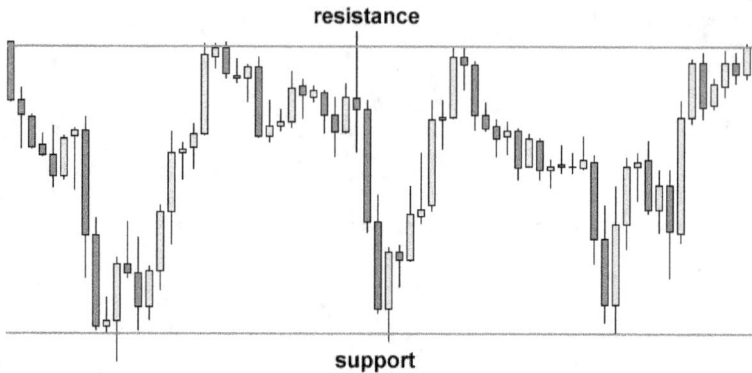

Features-

- Most of the time these patterns are bullish reversal or just a continuation pattern.

Explanation-

- Two equivalent highs and two equivalent lows are required to form the resistance and the support respectively.
- Similar to symmetrical pattern as both shows continuation, but rectangle pattern is not complete until a breakout has occurred.
- Direction of breakout usually cannot be predetermined.
- As the price nears support, buyers push the price higher, while on the other hand, as the prices nears resistance, sellers force the price lower.

Trading-

- Buy near support and sell near resistance.
- Short sell at resistance and cover up at support.

- One other way is there, though it has a good probability of occurrence, but not guaranteed-
    - Calculate the height or difference between the support and resistance. For example, Let support be at Rs 120 while resistance be at Rs 150. Thus the height is (150-120) = Rs 30.
    - Once the breakout takes place at Rs 150, you can set a target price of (150+30) = Rs 180.
    - It might take sum time to get to that level, so the traders are advised to remain patient.

Chapter 10: Case Studies

NOTE- Companies mentioned here are purely for educational purpose only and not for any promotional purpose. Readers are advised to do their own research and analysis before investing or trading.

In this chapter, we are going to analyse two real companies currently listed on stock exchanges (NSE and BSE). We will analyse just like the way we discussed earlier (basic fundamental analysis), we are going to check top line, bottom line, profit, share prices, splits, dividend history, volume etc. Your task is to compare these companies with each other and decide which one is better for investment.

Case Study 1

- **Name-** Britannia Industries Ltd.
- **Date-** 30th July, 2020
- **Time-** 14:45 hours
- **BSE-** Rs 3802.50 (Volume- 14874)
- **NSE-** Rs 3801.00 (Volume- 712970)
- **Market Capital-** Rs 92529.11 (Cr.)
- **Face Value-** Rs 1
- **5 year record-**

Year ->	2020	2019	2018	2017	2016
Top Line	11599.55	11054.67	9913.99	9054.09	8397.23
% change	4.92	11.50	9.49	7.82	-
Profit	11878.95	11261.12	10080.36	9204.63	8521.58
% change	5.48	11.70	9.51	8.01	-
Bottom Line	1393.16	1156.43	1004.14	884.33	824.36
% change	20.40	15.16	13.50	07.20	-
Share Price	2688.95	3096.55	2485.30	1697.58	1319.25
% change	-13.16	24.60	46.40	28.67	-

NOTE- All values mentioned in the table correspond to values at the end of March of their respective years.

- **Dividend History-**

Type	Percentage	Date
Interim	3500	29th April, 2020
Final	1500	1st August, 2019
Final	1250	27th July, 2018
Final	1100	28th July, 2017
Final	1000	29th July, 2016

- **Stock Split-**

Old FV	New FV	Date
2	1	29th November, 2018
10	2	8th September, 2010

- **Bonus-**

Ratio	Year
1:1	2018
1:2	1999
1:2	1989
2:5	1987
2:5	1983

- **Observations-**
> Fall of share price almost by 13.16% in the year 2020. Covid-19 pandemic situation's the reason.
> Numbers in the 5 year record chart are always increasing which shows that the company is stable and performs well.
> %change in share price from year 2018 to 2019 is much lower than that of from the year 2017 to 2018. This is because there has been a stock split in the year 2018. Still the share price in 2019 is greater than that of 2018. This is a positive indication.
> Changes in bottom line are much greater as compared to top line. That means that overall profit is greater than sales, which indicates that demand is increasing. This is

another very good and positive indication that share prices are going to increase in future as well.
- ➢ Gave a total return of 103.82% in last 5 years.
- ➢ Gave good amount of dividends every year for last 5 years, which is a plus point.
- ➢ Old share holders enjoy the benefits of bonus as well.

- **Conclusion-**
- ➢ Company's performances are stable.
- ➢ Good for investments.

Case Study 2

- **Name-** Yes Bank Ltd.
- **Date-** 31st July, 2020
- **Time-** 16:00 hours
- **BSE-** Rs 11.95 (Volume- 10312327)
- **NSE-** Rs 11.95 (Volume- 120256191)
- **Market Capital-** Rs 29940.61 (Cr.)
- **Face Value-** Rs 2
- **5 year record-**

Year	2020	2019	2018	2017	2016
Top Line	26052.02	29623.80	20268.59	16425.00	13533.44
% change	-12.05	46.15	23.40	21.36	-
Profit	38008.12	34299.27	25561.74	20642.80	16262.86
% change	10.81	34.18	23.82	26.93	-
Bottom Line	-16432.57	1709.26	4233.21	3339.88	2529.69
% change	-1061.38	-59.62	26.74	32.02	-
Share Price	24.90	276.10	304.85	308.99	173.26
% change	-90.98	-9.43	-1.33	78.33	-

NOTE- All values mentioned in the table correspond to values at the end of March of their respective years.

- **Dividend History-**

Type	Percentage	Date
Final	100	3rd June, 2019
Final	135	4th June, 2018
Final	120	29th May, 2017
Final	100	30th May, 2016
Final	90	21st Mat, 2015

- **Stock Split-**

Old FV	New FV	Date
10	2	21st September, 2017

- **Bonus-**
  No recent bonus.

- **NPA (Non Performing Assets)-**

Year	Percentage
2020	5.03
2019	2.00
2018	1.00
2017	1.00
2016	0.00

- **Observations-**
➤ Top Line in 2020 fell by 12.05% which is a very big number. Recall our discussion on stock analysis. For a good company, top line must be always increasing. A fall in top line is not at all a good indication.
➤ Although profit increased in 2020, but the bottom line fell by 1061.38%, which is truly a great number. The company faced a very big loss, as the company was involved in fraud activities, which were exposed in the year 2020. Even by the end of July of 2020, the share price fell near to Rs 4. A big negative point for the company.
➤ From the year 2018, share prices started falling and continued till date. Again not a favorable point for the company.

➢ Although the company gives dividends, but the numbers are not so big.

- **Conclusion-**

➢ Company's performance is very unstable.
➢ Not good for investments.

Case Study 3

- **Name-** State Bank of India.
- **Overview-**

Formerly known as Imperial Bank of India, SBI or State Bank of India is the largest public sector bank in India with a 23% market share by assets and a 25% share of the total loan and deposits market. As on 31st March 2017, Indian government held around 61.23% equity shares in SBI. Even LIC is the largest non-promoter shareholder in the company with 8.82% shareholding.

Shareholders	Shareholding
Promoters: Government of India	56.92%
FIIs/GDRs/OCBs/NRIs	10.94%
Banks & Insurance Companies	10.63%
Mutual Funds & UTI	13.72%
Others	07.79%
Total	100%

*Source- Wikipedia

After the Yes Bank scam share price of Yes Bank started falling drastically. As a part of RBI directed rescue deal on March 2020, State Bank of India acquired 48.2% of the shares of Yes Bank. Stay tuned, I will post a fundamental analysis report on Yes Bank very soon.

- **Date-** 10th August, 2020
- **Time-** 14:45 hours
- **BSE-** Rs 193.60 (Volume- 2551840)
- **NSE-** Rs 193.75 (Volume- 48762841)
- **Market Capital-** Rs 173048.22 (Cr.)
- **Face Value-** Rs 1
- **5 year record-** (in Rs cr.)

Year ->	2020	2019	2018	2017	2016
Top Line	269851.66	253322.14	228970.28	230447.49	221854.84
% change	6.52	10.63	-0.64	3.87	-
Profit	368010.64	330220.88	306527.52	298640.45	272871.02
% change	11.44	7.73	2.64	9.44	-
Bottom Line	18176.81	2602.59	-4176.73	-387.02	12747.34
% change	598.41	162.31	-979.20	-103.03	-
Share Price	196.85	320.75	249.90	293.40	194.25
% change	-38.6	28.35	-14.82	51.04	-

NOTE- All values mentioned in the table correspond to values at the end of March of their respective years.

- **Stock Split-**

Old FV	New FV	Date
10	1	November, 2014

- **Dividend History-**

Type	Percentage	Date
Final	260.00	26th May, 2017
Final	260.00	3rd June, 2016
Final	350.00	28th May, 2015
Final	150.00	29th May, 2014
Interim	150.00	11th March, 2014

- **Bonus-** No bonus is last 5 years.

- **NPA (Non Performing Assets)-**

Year	Percentage
2020	2.23
2019	3.00
2018	6.00
2017	4.00
2016	4.00

- **Observations-**
  - Decline of share price by almost 38.6% in the year 2020. Covid-19 pandemic situation's the reason.
  - For a stable company top line must be always increasing. But From year 2017 to

- 2018 top line reduced by 0.64%, which is not a good indication.
- Percentage increases of top line and profit in other years are not so good as compared to other banks like HDFC.
- Considering the bottom line data, in year 2017 and 2018 SBI faced huge loses. Bottom line must be always increasing at a rate greater than top line. But here the case is not at all favorable.
- Share price even fell by 14.82% in the year 2018, again a negative factor for SBI.
- Didn't issue any dividend since 2017.
- NPAs are also very high as compared to some other banks. In 2018, NPA was 6% which is a very big number. SBI faced huge losses in 2018.

- **Conclusion-**
- Although SBI is India's largest public sector bank its performances are not stable.
- Not a good company for investments.

Case Study 4

- **Name-** Mahindra and Mahindra Ltd.
- **Overview-**

Established in 1945 Mahindra and Mahindra is an Indian multinational vehicle manufacturing company. It is the largest tractor manufacturing company in the world and one of the largest vehicle manufacturing companies in India. Mahindra and Mahindra produces SUVs, sedans, pickup trucks, lightweight and heavyweight commercial vehicles, motorcycles and tractors. It also has a global presence and exports its products to many countries.

M&M took a 55% stake in REVA Electric in 2010 and renamed it to Mahindra Electric in 2016 following taking 100% ownership. In 2011 it acquired South Korea's SsangYong Motor Company. In October 2014, it acquired a 51% controlling stake in Peugeot Motorcycles and 100% in October 2019. During the same time, Mahindra entered into a joint venture with Ford by establishing Ford India in which Mahindra acquired a controlling stake of 51%.

Stock Market: Build Your Basics

- **Date-** 21st August, 2020
- **Time-** 16:00 hours
- **BSE-** Rs 611.25 (Volume- 114635)
- **NSE-** Rs 609.80 (Volume- 4191443)
- **Market Capital-** Rs 75990.14 (Cr.)
- **Face Value-** Rs 5
- **5 year record-** (in Rs cr.)

Year ->	2020	2019	2018	2017	2016
Top Line	95179.09	104720.68	92093.95	83773.05	75841.42
% change	-9.11	13.71	9.93	10.45	-
Profit	96241.68	105806.29	92724.98	84503.15	76362.47
% change	-9.03	14.10	9.72	10.66	-
Bottom Line	-1363.58	4650.33	6850.53	3151.13	2708.47
% change	-129.32	-32.11	117.32	16.34	-
Share Price	274.40	673.90	738.90	643.45	605.35
% change	-59.28	-8.79	14.83	6.29	-

NOTE- All values mentioned in the table correspond to values at the end of March of their respective years.

- **Stock Split-**

Old FV	New FV	Date
10	5	29th March, 2010

- **Dividend History-**

Type	Percentage	Date
Final	47.00	16th July, 2020
Final	170.00	18th July, 2019
Final	150.00	12th July, 2018
Final	260.00	13th July, 2017
Final	240.00	21st July, 2016

- **Bonus-**

Ratio	Year
1:1	2017
1:1	2005
2:3	1995
2:3	1984
1:1	1980

- **Observations-**

➢ M&M comes under Sensex and Nifty50.

➢ Good amount of dividends are provided to shareholders every year, even in the pandemic situation of 2020.

➢ Till 2018, the change in bottom line was greater as compared to top line, which was a good indication till 2019. In the year 2019, due to the introduction of BSVI regulations by the government, M&M faced huge

losses. Also in 2020, due to the pandemic condition share price declined drastically.
- ➢ M&M faced losses but only due to temporary outside conditions.

- **Conclusion-**
- ➢ Company's performances were affected only by temporary conditions, from which the company can recover easily. New models of M&M meet the regulations of BSVI.
- ➢ A good company for investment.

Case Study 5

- **Name-** Asian Paints Ltd.
- **Overview-**

Asian Paints Ltd. an Indian multinational company engaged in manufacturing, selling and distribution of paints and related products. It is India's largest and Asia's third largest paints corporation. It had the largest market share with 54.1% in the Indian paint industry by the year 2015.

Asian Paints is one of the top performing companies in India and is included in both Sensex and Nifty50.

- **Date-** 15th August, 2020
- **Time-** 20:40 hours
- **BSE-** Rs 1801.60 (Volume- 209020)
- **NSE-** Rs 1802.55 (Volume- 1868406)
- **Market Capital-** Rs 172809.07 (Cr.)
- **Face Value-** Rs 1

- **5 year record-** (in Rs cr.)

Year ->	2020	2019	2018	2017	2016
Top Line	20221.25	19240.13	16824.55	15061.99	14271.49
% change	5.09	14.35	11.70	5.53	-
Profit	20515.56	19437.17	17045.17	15324.42	14484.88
% change	5.54	14.03	11.2	5.79	-
Bottom Line	2728.40	2173.11	1981.73	1940.78	1769.36
% change	25.55	9.65	2.10	9.68	-
Share Price	1594.95	1497.00	1131.10	1073.50	881.85
% change	6.54	32.34	5.36	21.73	-

NOTE- All values mentioned in the table correspond to values at the end of March of their respective years.

- **Stock Split-**

Old FV	New FV	Date
10	1	July, 2013

- **Dividend History-**

Type	Percentage	Date
Final	150	23rd July, 2020
Interim	715	3rd March, 2020
Interim	335	30th October, 2019
Final	765	13th June, 2019
Interim	285	29th October, 2018

- **Bonus-**

Ratio	Year
1:2	2003
3:5	2000
1:1	1995

- **Observations-**
  - Top line is always increasing, even during the pandemic situation of 2020 its top line increased by 5.09% which is a positive indication.
  - Profit, bottom line and share price are also increasing.
  - Volume of trade is also high, which reduces the risk.
  - Gave an average compounded annual return of nearly 16%.
  - The company also gives good amount of dividend, both interim and final.
  - The company is even listed in Sensex and Nifty50, which ensures company's good performance.

- **Conclusion-**
  - ➢ Company's performances are stable.
  - ➢ Good company for investments.

This is how basic analysis of companies is done. Also put considerable focus on future prospects or plans of companies. I would recommend readers to now try to and practice analysis of some companies on their own. You can even start with companies which are similar to those discussed here, like Nestle is similar to Britannia, HDFC bank is similar to Yes bank.

Chapter 11: Buffet's Rules

"You don't need to be a rocket scientist. Investing is not a game where the guy with 160 IQ beats the guy with 130 IQ. Rationality is essential."

-Warren Buffett

Warren Buffett's 7 rules of investing-

Rule 1: When you buy shares, try to hold it forever-

Warren Buffett always talks about the power of compound interest. When you buy and hold shares for a longer time, share prices increase and your net worth gets compounded annually. Some of us try to sell the shares at a very early stage, say within a few months, or maybe a year for short term profits or returns. This constant buying and selling of shares disrupts the game play of compound interest and sufficient return is not achieved.

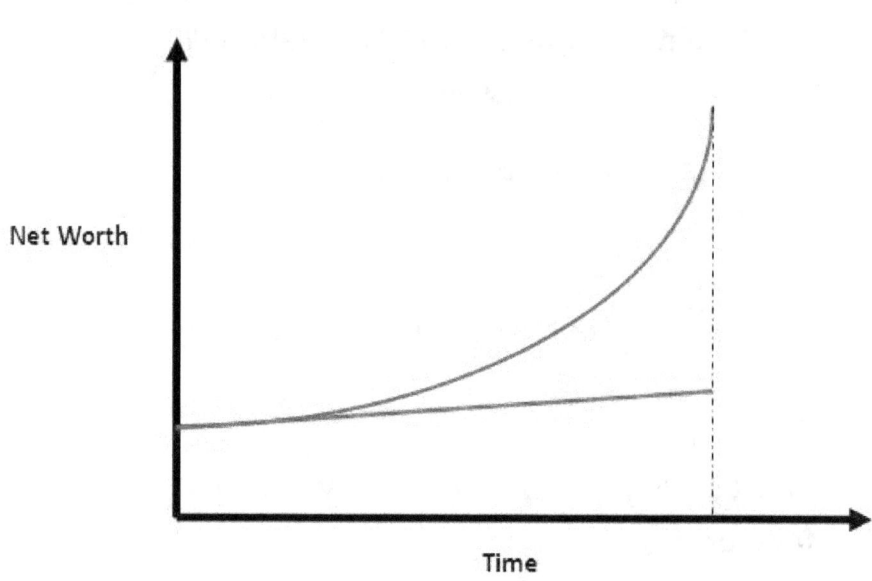

Rule 2: If the business performs well, the stocks will eventually follow-

Simple rule, yet confusing for many investors. The moment we shares are bought, some investors start to panic, whether share price are going rise up or decline. Think about a scenario where the demand for onions in the market is greater than its supply. What do you think will happen? Of course price of onions will rise. Similarly, if the company in which you have invested performs well, then naturally the share price will rise and vice versa.

Rule 3: Take advice from experts and those you know and trust-

You cannot enter the market without any knowledge about it. You cannot afford to invest blindly in any company. You need to have some basic knowledge about investing. And here comes the importance of mentors. According to Buffett, one should seek advice from experts or mentors whom he trusts. Fake mentors often give fake advices which lead to great financial loses.

Benjamin Graham, author of the famous book, "The Intelligent Investor", is considered to be the father of value investing. Warren Buffett was one of Graham's students at Columbia Business School.

Rule 4: Most news are not necessary, they are just noise-

Many investors spend their whole day listening to stock market news. Well there is nothing wrong about it, but if you notice carefully, most of those news are unnecessary. In order to gain more popularity and more viewers news channels often discuss on very advance level topics regarding the market which are not actually required to understand the market. Those are not news, but noise. Investors start to panic which often leads to wrong decisions. Ignore the noise, focus on the news only.

Rule 5: Buy shares of those companies which you understand-

Understanding the company is very important. Before we decide to invest in a particular company, we must analyse it. If you don't know how the company makes money, you cannot predict whether the share price is going to rise or fall. Suppose you want to invest in a textile company, but you have absolutely no idea how the textile industry or that company works. In such scenarios, you are most likely to buy shares of the wrong company. Try to understand the business first. Even Buffett invests in companies which are very simple to understand, like "Coca Cola".

Rule 6: Be fearful when others become greedy and vice versa-

Sometimes, there comes a sudden rise in the demand for shares of a company, which leads to sudden rise in the share price. Investors become greedy and start buying shares hoping that share price will rise up might even get overvalued. This is the time when smart investors avoid any investments. They know that such scenarios are temporary and a sudden decline in the share price will take place. Once the price rise hits the saturation, price starts falling rapidly, and most investor start selling their shares. This often causes the share price gets undervalued. This is the time when smart investors become greedy and make their moves. They get the opportunity to buy shares at a very low price, which gives them much more profit in the long run.

Rule 7: Try to buy stocks below its intrinsic value-

Buffett says,

"No company, no matter how wonderful, is worthy an infinite price. Price is what you pay, value is what you get!"

A very common mistake investors make is that they buy stocks of those companies which are very trending, whose share prices are already very high. That is not the way smart investors invest. The key rule of investing in- "Buy Low, Sale High". If you buy shares at very a high price, you actually lose the opportunity to maximize your profit. Buffett suggests buying shares at or close to their intrinsic value or at a price that they are actually worth. Today if onions are worth Rs 20 per kilo and tomorrow if the price rises suddenly to Rs 200 per kilo, are you going to buy onions @ Rs 200? Or wait for some more days for the price to fall again to Rs 20 or near to Rs 20? Similar is the case with shares. Always try to buy shares at their intrinsic value.

Chapter 12: Important Notes

- **Selecting the right broker-** there are several stock brokers out there. I recommend my readers to go for online stock brokers over traditional brokers. This is because intraday trading becomes much easier on online platform, brokerage charges are much lower than traditional brokers. It also saves time. I am not promoting any broker; it is your personal decision. But before you start with one, always check its SEBI registration number (SEBI for India). It is mandatory for brokers in India to have their unique SEBI registration number. Once you select a broker, verify its SEBI registration number on the website of SEBI. It is always recommended that you choose a broker who is well known and well reputed.
- **What if your broker runs away-** immediately inform SEBI about this. SEBI is very strict in such scenarios and takes measures immediately.

- **Beware of scams and fraud calls-** many times brokers call their clients and insist them to buy shares of a company. Don't fall in such traps. They might perform **boiler room scams**, where brokers first buy shares of companies which are either unstable, or at the verge of bankruptcy, whose share prices are very low (penny stocks). Later on those brokers force their clients to place buy orders for stocks of those companies. As a result of which share prices rise rapidly and become overpriced. The moment it happens, brokers sell all of their shares at such high prices. As a result of which share prices starts falling rapidly and investors face huge losses. Never be a victim of such scams. Always study and analyse before you invest.
- **Never put all your eggs in one basket-** it is a very common phrase used in the market. Experts always suggest that investors must diversify their portfolio or in simple words must invest in various companies rather than investing in a single company. This reduces the risk.

- **Types of orders-** while investing or trading through online brokers, you will come across several types of orders for buying and selling of stock, like market order, bracket order, cover order, etc. Types of orders offered by brokers vary from broker to broker. I suggest you to first do your own research before selecting your broker and then learn about the orders offered by the broker. Learn about all the orders in details before making any investment.
- **Right time for trading-** when the market opens, you might notice very high volatility in share prices. This is because all the orders placed during aftermarket hours get executed when the market opens. Beginners are usually advised to avoid trading during this period as the market becomes very unpredictable.
- **Indian market opening time-** 09.15 am. (Monday-Friday)
- **Indian market closing time-** 03.30 pm. (Monday- Friday)

Chapter 13: Mutual Funds

A mutual fund is a type of financial instrument where a pool of money is collected from individual investors and invested in securities like stocks, bonds, debentures, certificates of deposits and other assets.

Mutual funds are operated and managed by professionals, who invest the fund in various securities and attempt to produce capital gain for the investors. A share of a mutual fund represents investments in many different stocks or other securities instead of just one holding.

Types of Mutual Funds-

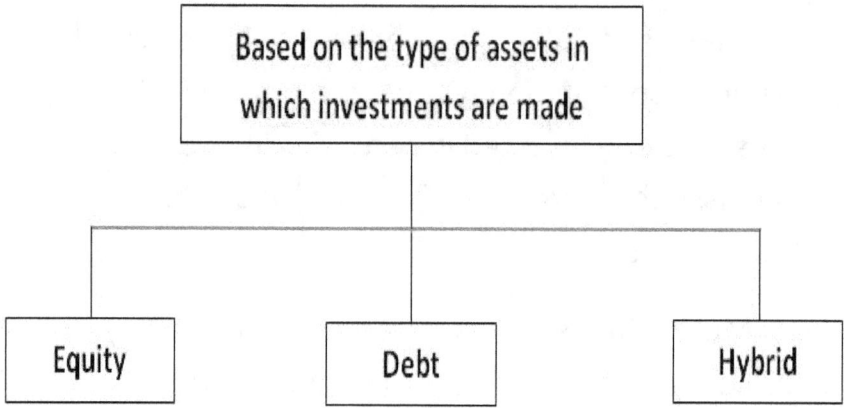

Let's have a discussion on and understand each of them-

Equity Funds

Those mutual funds which invest in the stock market are known as equity mutual funds or equity funds.

Types of equity funds-

1. Large cap fund
2. Mid cap fund
3. Small cap fund
4. Sector fund
5. Diversified equity fund
6. Dividend yield fund
7. Thematic fund
8. Equity Linked Savings Scheme (ELSS)

- **Large cap fund-** based on market capitalization companies can be categorized as large cap, mid cap and small cap companies. Ranges for market cap for each category changes from time to time. Equity funds which invest in large cap companies are called large cap mutual funds. Large cap companies are stable and well established, hence involve lesser risk.

- **Mid cap fund-** Equity funds which invest in mid cap companies are called mid cap mutual funds.
- **Small cap fund-** Equity funds which invest in small cap companies are called small cap mutual funds. Small cap companies are generally those companies which are new in the market or not very stable, hence involves good amount of risk. At the same time many small cap companies have very high potential for performance, in such cases small cap funds might give much higher returns as compared to large cap or mid cap funds.
- **Sector fund-** Equity funds which invest in a particular sector only. For example, 'Reliance Media and Entertainment Fund' invests in media and entertainment sector only.
- **Diversified equity fund-** Equity funds which invest in various sectors and in different

market caps are known as diversified equity fund. Diversified equity funds involve lesser amount of risk as it diversifies its portfolio.
- **Dividend yield fund-** Equity funds which invest in companies which are stable, consistent and give regular dividends to share holders are known as dividend yield bonds.
- **Thematic fund-** Equity funds which invest in themes are known as thematic funds. For example, 'HDFC Housing Opportunities Fund' whose theme is 'housing', hence buys shares of those companies which are related to housing like cement companies, paint companies etc.
- **Equity Linked Savings Scheme-** ELSS is a tax saver scheme whose minimum investment period is 3 years. Under Section 80C of Income Tax Act. Investors can claim a tax benefit of up to Rs 1.5 lakh.

ELSS Features-

- Investors must invest for a minimum period of 3 years before taking back their money.
- Tax exemption up to Rs 1.5 Lakh on returns.
- Income after 3 years is considered to be LTCG and taxed at 10% if the income is over 1 Lakh.
- No maximum tenure period.
- Investor's money is invested in a diversified manner, across different market cap and sectors.
- A minimum of 80% of the total fund is invested in equity.

Debt Funds

Mutual funds which invest in debentures, bonds, certificate of deposits and other debt instruments are known as debt funds. Debt instruments are generally used to borrow money from individual investors just like loans from banks. Debt funds involve lesser risk and give lesser returns as compared to equity funds.

Types of debt funds-

1. Gilt fund
2. Junk bond schemes
3. Fixed maturity plans
4. Liquid fund/schemes

- **Gilt fund-** such funds invest in government securities only. Since these securities are issued by government, they involve absolutely zero risks.
- **Junk bond schemes-** junk bonds are issued by companies which are struggling financially. Junk bond schemes invest in such bonds. Junk bond schemes carry very high risks which are compensated by higher interest rates.
- **Fixed maturity plan-** these are similar to bank fixed deposits. Such funds invest in corporate bonds, certificates and commercial papers. Returns of fixed maturity plans are better than bank fixed deposits.
- **Liquid fund/schemes-** liquid funds invest in money market instruments like certificates

of deposits, treasury bills, commercial papers, term deposits etc. Such money market instruments borrow money for a very short period of time from investors. Liquid funds involve lesser risk and lesser volatility as compared to other schemes. Also, investors can take out their money anytime they wish. Liquid funds/schemes are best for short term investments.

Hybrid Funds

As the name suggests, such mutual funds invest in both equity and debt funds. Equity funds give higher returns and involve greater risk as compared to debt funds. Thus in hybrid funds, by investing in both equity and debt funds an attempt is made to balance the risk and increase the return.

Types of hybrid funds-

1. Monthly income plan
2. Balanced fund
3. Arbitrage fund

- **Monthly Income Plan-** 60% to 90% of investor's money is invested in debt instruments. The rest is invested in equities. Since most of the money is invested in debt instruments, monthly income plans are safer than equity funds.
- **Balanced fund-** 65% to 85% of investor's money is invested in equities and the rest in debt instruments.
- **Arbitrage fund-** more than 65% of investor's money is invested in equity. One benefit of arbitrage fund is that the principle amount remains safe.

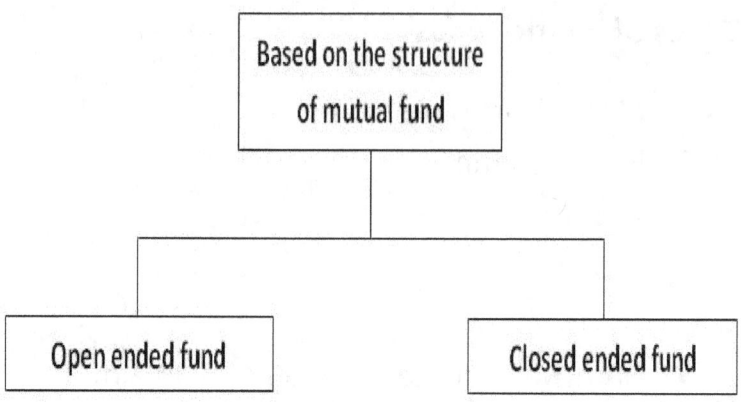

Open ended fund- investors can buy or sell units at anytime they wish.

Closed ended fund- these schemes involves fixed maturity periods. Investors can take out their money only after maturity.

Chapter 14: Scams

Investing in stock market, no doubt, is quite a big deal for beginners. Some rookie investors even invest blindly, without doing any personal analysis. Some invest in those companies which are suggested by their relatives or the stock broker. WARNING!!!! Before you invest, complete your own analysis first.

Lack of knowledge might result in huge losses for investors. Some fraud stock brokers use this opportunity to manipulate your decision, use your money to manipulate the market, and at the end, enjoy your money as their profit, while you lose all your money.

As an investor, you must be aware of such scams or frauds. In this chapter we will discuss about two very famous real-life scams which had great impacts on the entire stock market system.

1. <u>Jordan Belfort Scam</u> (Pump and Dump Scam)

Have you watched the famous movie *The Wolf of Wall Street*? Though most of the people out there watch the movie for its explicit scenes only, lol, but the movie is actually based on a stock market scam. Jordan Belfort was the mastermind behind the scam. The movie is an adaptation of the book *The Wolf of Wall Street*, written by Jordan Belfort himself.

To understand the scam, let's first have a quick look at the background of Jordan Belfort. Born in 9th July, 1962, Jordan Ross Belfort completed his graduation from American University with a degree in biology. Soon after, Belfort started a meat selling business in New York. It had an initial success, but ultimately failed when he was 25. Later on with the help of a family friend, he found a job as a trainee stockbroker at L.F.Rothschild. But due to the stock market crash of 1987 he lost his job.

Stratton Oakmont and the Scam

Belfort started his own stock broking company Stratton Oakmont as a franchise of Stratton Securities, then later bought out the original founder. Belfort was an expert at convincing his potential clients or investors to buy shares of any company. First, he suggests his clients to buy shares of pretty good companies, which give them pretty high returns. Satisfied customers now start trusting Belfort and Stratton Oakmont. Now, here Belfort uses a strategy what is known as **Boiler Room**, where investors are defrauded with the "pump and dump" type stock sales. Stratton Oakmont targets and manipulates Penny Stocks.

Penny Stocks are stocks of those companies which are at the verge of bankruptcy. Price of those stocks are generally very low and are often not listed on the stock exchange. These stocks are traded over-the-counter, that is, directly from seller to buyer via a broker.

Stratton Oakmont first buys all the stocks such a company at a very very low price. Since such companies are not listed, very less information is available about them. Belfort misuses this opportunity. He writes a beautiful script about the company, giving false information like it has a high potential for growth, high growth rate in past financial years, etc. Employees of Stratton Oakmont then use this script to convince investors to invest heavily in that company. Since Belfort already has their trust, investors start investing blindly.

When more and more investors start placing buying orders, prices of the stocks increase rapidly. Once the prices are considerably high, Stratton Oakmont books the profit and sells all its shares and stops promoting the company. This sudden selling of shares drops the share price rapidly. While investors face huge losses, Belfort and his employees enjoys all the profit. Since this whole activity was illegal, Belfort used to put all his money in Swiss Bank.

Belfort's Lifestyle

Belfort developed a lifestyle that consisted of lavish parties, big real estates, exotic cars and yacht and what not. At the age of 26, he was millionaire, making $50 million a year. He once generated a hotel bill of $700,000. You can watch more of his craziness in the movie. He valued his employees as well and often used to throw parties and payed them well to keep them happy and satisfied. Meanwhile, Belfort also developed his addiction for drugs.

Downfall of Stratton Oakmont

While Belfort was enjoying his fortune, Stratton Oakmont was under constant scrutiny from National Association of Securities Dealers from 1989 onward. Finally in December 1996, NASD expelled Stratton Oakmont. In 1999, Belfort pleaded guilty to securities fraud and money laundering. In 2003, Belfort was sentenced to four years in prison and personally fined $110 million. He cooperated with the authorities and exposed his partners, which shortened his prison sentenced to 22 months. In prison Belfort met comedian Tommy Chong, who gave him the idea of writing down his story.

Life after Prison

After his release, Belfort published his memoir *The Wolf of Wall Street* in 2008, on which the 2013 movie *The Wolf of Wall Street* is based on. Belfort released his second memoir *Catching the Wolf of Wall Street*. Belfort now operates his own company Straight Line, which provides sales and marketing training. He also gives motivational speeches worldwide.

2. **Harshad Mehta Scam**

The name, Harshad Mehta is quite famous now a days, not only for the mind blowing series *Scam 1992: The Harshad Mehta Story* from Sony Liv, but also for India's Biggest Stock Market Scam.

Early Life and Interest in Stock Market

Harshad Shantilal Mehta was born on 29th July, 1954 at Paneli Moti, Rajkot district of Gujrat. He completed his B.Com from Mumbai's Lala Lajput Rai College and worked a number of odd jobs for the next eight years.

Meanwhile, Harshad's interest in the stock market grew and joined B Ambalal broker, and later joined stock broker J.L. Shah and Nandalal Sheth.

Harshad was really wise at understanding the Market. He used to gather inside information from companies and use them wisely in trading. His success made him quite famous in the Bombay Stock Exchange in no time. Other traders started trusting him and traded in companies suggested by Harshad.

Grow More Research and Asset Management

In 1984, along with his brother, Harshad started his stock broking company Grow More Research and Asset Management, and became a broker for Bombay Stock Exchange (BSE).

The business was running quite well, but Harshad wanted to take it to a step further. He wanted to enter in the money market. This initiated the Scam.

Ready Forward Deal

Before we understand the scam, one must understand the concept of **Ready Forward Deal** (RF Deals), because RF deals were the main source of funds for Harshad's scam.

In order to raise funds for its expenses, Government issues **Government Securities,** such as government bonds, and in return pays interests to its investors. In those days, it was mandatory for banks to invest in those securities.

Securities can also be used for getting short term loans. When a bank needs a short term loan, it sells its securities to another bank and gets a short term loan. Later on it returns the money to the lending bank along with interest and gets back its securities. This is known as a Ready Forward Deal.

Note that, in RF deals, instead of giving away the securities directly, banks give Bank Receipts (BRs), which is a mean of confirmation that for both the banks that securities has been transferred from the selling bank to the buying bank.

But, such deals have to be done via a broker. A broker acts as an intermediator, whose job is to find buyer for the bank who wants to sell its securities. And here comes the role of Harshad Mehta.

Beginning of the Scam

Harshad now entered the money market and became a broker for ready forward deals. As per the guidelines of RBI (Reserve Bank of India), the cheque issued by the security buying bank must be issued in the name of the security selling bank.

Harshad Mehta was a well reputed and trustworthy broker at that time. So, Harshad used to convince banks to issue cheques in his name and give him some time to find buyers and sellers for the securities.

Once Harshad gets the money, he then starts the real scam. Since the cheques were issued in his name, he used the money to invest heavily in the stock market and manipulate the same. Since Harshad was very successful and famous in the stock market, other investors used to invest in those companies in which he used to invest.

Harshad's heavy investments in the stock market brought a bull run. Share prices started increasing rapidly. He even raised the share price of *ACC* from Rs200 to Rs9000 in a very short span of time. When the share prices were significantly high, Harshad used to book his profit and sell his shares.

Leaving behind his profit, he then used to give the rest of the money to the security selling bank and the securities to the security buying bank and the matter used to get settled. In this way, Harshad used the funds of banks to manipulate the stock market.

Harshad took the scam to a higher level. With the help of some smaller banks, Harshad started making fake BRs, and used them to raise funds from banks for his investments.

Explanation with Example

Let us understand this by an example. Let, Bank A wants to sell its securities in return of X amount of money. Harshad Mehta now comes into the picture. He takes the securities from Bank A and asks for some time to find a buyer. Let, Bank B be the buyer, who will buy the securities.

Harshad now convinces Bank B to issue a cheque of X amount in his name and asks for some time give to deliver the securities to Bank B. Once Harshad gets the cheque of X amount, he invests it in the stock market.

From the stock market, after selling his shares, he gets a profit of Y amount. So, the total amount of capital he has now is (X+Y). Harshad then gives Bank A the money it required, i.e. X and gives Bank B the securities, and enjoys a profit of Y amount.

Downfall of Harshad and its Impact on the Market

Everything was going fine, till the stock market strike in 1992. Harshad had already invested a lot of money in the market, but due to the strike market remained closed for several days, This made Harshad face huge losses as he had to pay the banks from his pocket. The situations became worse and Harshad found it difficult to pay the money to the designated banks.

Meanwhile, on 23rd April 1992 Sucheta Dalal, a journalist and reporter of Times of India exposed the scam, which became another burden for Harshad. On 9th November, 1992 CBI arrested Harshad and charged with a total of 600 Civil Action Suits and 70 Criminal Cases. SEBI banned Harshad from entering the stock market for lifetime.

Eventually the market crashed. Index fell by 12.77%, which is the largest fall in history. The banking sector faced a loss of Rs4000 crore, which was a huge amount for 1992. You can now very well imagine the situations of small individual investors.

Moral

Dear reader, stock market scams are very common. But that doesn't mean that you will be a victim of such a scam. You are an *intelligent investor*. After going through those case studies tell me what you can make out of it?

In both the cases, investors were affected the most. In the Belfort case, he targeted individual investors directly, while in Harshad's case, individual investors were affected indirectly.

Now, if you think carefully, you will observe that investors invested blindly in companies suggested by these frauds, and eventually faced the consequences. The main purpose of this chapter is to make you understand the importance of personal analysis of companies before investing in them. For example, in the case of Belfort, he used to manipulate penny stocks. And we know that investing in penny stocks involves huge amount of risk. If investors had done their personal analysis before investing, they wouldn't have faced such poor consequences. Similarly, in Harshad's case, the share price of ACC was overvalued; the P/E ratio was too high, still investors invested in ACC, since Harshad was a reputed broker and everybody wanted to be rich like him. When the scam was exposed, the market crashed very badly. The loss was huge, even some innocent investors committed suicide.

Dear reader, recall that chapter where we discussed about some myths regarding the stock market. Yes investing is risky, but only when you invest blindly. So, when you start investing, I request you to please analyse thoroughly before putting your money in.

Tip and Recommendation Call Fraud

Apart from pump and dump scams, there is one other scam, which is quite famous nowadays. This is called Tip and Recommendation Call Fraud.

There are some companies which provide tips and recommendations to investors in return of some money. They call you and give you tips and suggest you companies in which you should invest.

Though some of these companies are genuine and provide quality information, but others misuse this opportunity. They call you, and claim to have very high tip accuracy, more than 90%. Even Warren Buffett's accuracy is not so high. Anyway, innocent investors still become their victims.

Such companies call you, and ask you to buy their membership and they will give you stock tips and recommendations regularly. Some investors ask them for free trial. Some companies straight away deny giving trial tips, but others provide free trial tips, from which the real game starts.

First, they target a handful of investors, say 100 investors. Among those 100 investors, they ask 50 of them to buy shares of a company, and the rest 50 to sell the shares of the same company. Evidently, one group of them will get profit and the other will lose. Now among those happy 50 investors, the company again asks 25 of them to buy and the other 25 to sell. Again, one group of them will get the profit. Now these 25 investors with profit start trusting the tip company and purchase their plan or membership. Later on when they start realizing what has actually happened, it is already too late.

Again, in this case also, investors become victims of such frauds due to lack of personal analysis. Do analysis yourself. Have faith and confidence in yourself and your analytical skills.

Extras

E1: Bonds

A bond is nothing but simply lending money to a company. Many a time, companies, which are not yet listed on the stock market, need huge capital for their operations. Newly established companies encounter such kind of situations. Since they are new, banks often refuses to give them loan. Thus companies start selling bonds.

But there are some fundamental differences between stocks and bonds-

1. Unlike stocks, if you buy any bond, you are simply lending money to the company and not buying a share of the company.
2. Since you are not buying any share, therefore the annual profit of the share has nothing to do with you.
3. The company returns your money with interest, just like a loan. These interest rates are often higher than the interest rates that a bank provides to its account holders.

4. In case the company goes bankrupt, it is mandatory for the company to return the money taken as bonds.
5. Prices of bonds are considerably higher than share prices.

E2: Terminology

- **Par Value-** or the face value is the price of each bond. Investors need to pay this price to buy a bond.
- **Discount-** bonds are often traded at discounted price.
- **Premium-** sometimes bonds are traded at a price higher than the par value or face value. For example, if face value is $1,000 and it is traded at $1,050, then it said to be trading at a premium of $50.
- **Coupon rate interest-** it is the rate of interest the company promises to pay the bondholder. It may be paid annually or semiannually.
- **Maturity-** it is the length of time until the bond comes due and the bondholder gets the par value of the bond.
- **Bid Price-** highest price that buyers will pay for the bond.
- **Ask Price-** lowest price offered by sellers for the bond.

- **Spread-** difference between the bid price and the ask price.

E3: IPO Analysis

Although investing in IPOs is generally not done by beginners, yet one should have some knowledge about it.

IPO stands for Initial Public Offering. When a private company wants to list itself on the stock exchange for the first time, it issues IPO. IPO in simple words refers to the shares of the company when it gets listed for the first time. One can buy these shares but with some rules.

Unlike in normal cases, where an investor can buy or sell any random number of shares, for investing in IPOs, investors cannot do that. Instead they need to buy shares in lots. Each lot has specified number of shares.

Also, since a lot of investors participate in IPOs, there is a complex method of lot allotment, which might sound too complicated for the time being, so just skip that part.

Now the question is, should you invest in IPOs or not. Well, some IPOs perform very well in future; some others go bankrupt in next few year. So, how to make sure that the IPO you have selected is going to perform well or not? Of course, no one can predict the future, but we can minimize our risks thorough analysis.

Just like we learned before, start your analysis by going through the company's financial statements. Try to make sure that all the ratios are good, make sure that top line and bottom line, both are increasing in past few years.

After doing all the fundamental analysis, now comes the question, why is the company launching its IPO? Why does it need to make the company public? Of course to raise more funds, but why the company needs more funds? That is the most important question.

To answer that question, let us understand the concept of **fresh issue** and **offer for sale**.

IPO = Fresh Issue + Offer for Sale

Through an IPO, a company raises funds by two methods-

1. **Fresh Issue (FI)-** Capital raised through fresh issues will be used by the company for its operations.
2. **Offer for Sale (OFS)-** If promoters, private equity investors are selling a part of their stake through offer for sale.

Before you invest in an IPO, make sure you check those parameters as well. There can be two cases-

1. **OFS>FI-** When OFS is greater than FI, that raises a red flag. If the promoters of the company want to sell their shares so early that might indicate that they know that the company is not going to survive, and thus sell their shares, book their profit and exit early.
2. **FI>OFS-** When FI is greater than OFS, that might indicate that the promoters of the company have faith and confidence on the company's performance and growth, hence not sell their shares for more profit in the future.

Also, don't forget to check the objective for fresh issue. There can be basically 4 objectives for fresh issue-

1. **Business expansion-** some companies raise funds to expand their business, which means that the company is absolutely confident about its growth in future. This is a positive indication.
2. **Acquisition of companies-** due to increase in competition, some well establish companies raise funds to buy smaller companies at the early stage to reduce market competition. Again, a positive sign.
3. **Debt repayment-** some companies raise funds to repay its short term debts. A very poor indication here.
4. **Working capital requirements-** some companies raise funds for its working capital, to keep their business running, which indicates that the cash flow system of the company is not stable. Again not a good sign.

That's all for now, I hope you enjoyed the book and learnt a lot about the stock market. Don't wait anymore, start your analysis and investing. Make sure you analyse thoroughly and very carefully. Never invest in a company which your emotions tell you to, but invest in a company in which your practical mind and analytical results tell you.

Money is a game, which is played by practical thinking and not by emotions.

Don't forget to share this book with your friends and family, share your knowledge with them. You can also visit my blog:

www.financiology21.blogspot.com

...The End...

www.ingramcontent.com/pod-product-compliance
Lightning Source LLC
Chambersburg PA
CBHW071403210526
45465CB00001B/228